A Garfield Christmas

BY: JIM DAVIS

BALLANTINE BOOKS • NEW YORK

A GARFIELD CHRISTMAS is based on the television special written by
Jim Davis, directed by Phil Roman, in association with United Media-
Mendelson Productions © 1987 United Feature Syndicate, Inc.

Library of Congress Catalog Card Number: 87-91371

ISBN: 0-345-35368-4

Manufactured in the United States of America

First Edition: December 1987

10 9 8 7 6 5 4 3 2 1

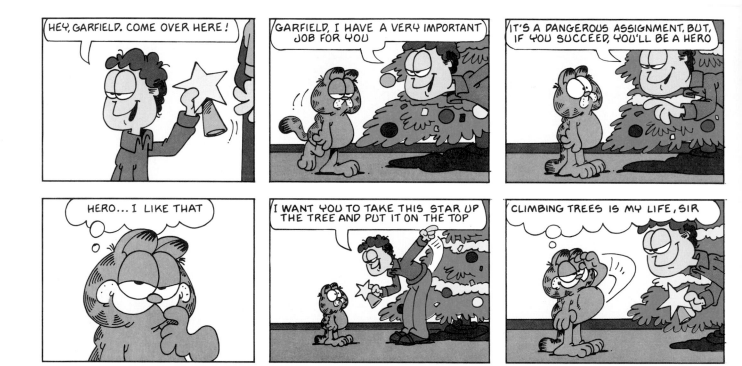

WHY, HELLO, GARFIELD. HOW DID YOU KNOW I NEEDED A KITTY IN MY LAP?

WILD GUESS

SINCE GRANDPA PASSED ON I'VE WHILED AWAY MANY A LONELY HOUR ROCKING AND STROKING MY CATS

I ENVY THOSE CATS

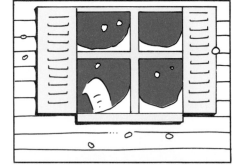

I DON'T BELIEVE IT. THESE LETTERS MUST BE 50 YEARS OLD

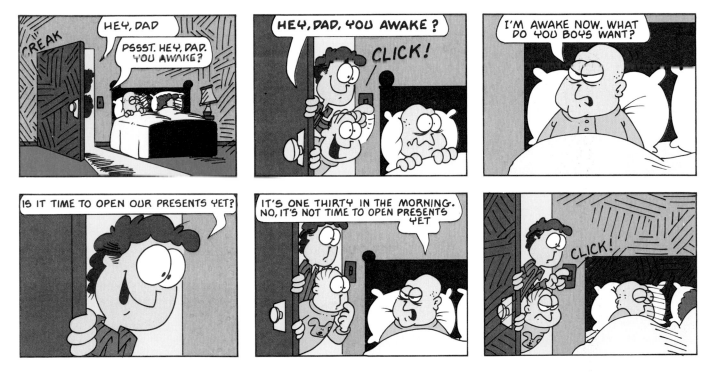

WHAT HAPPENED? DID YOU BOYS OVERSLEEP OR SOMETHING?

SOMEONE TURNED OUR ALARM CLOCK OFF

I KNOW

WELL, WHAT DO YOU BOYS WANT TO DO FIRST? DO YOU WANT TO DO CHORES, DO YOU WANT TO EAT BREAKFAST, OR DO YOU WANT TO OPEN PRESENTS?

PRESENTS!